The Entrepreneur's Blueprint

A Step-by-Step Guide to
Starting a New Business

J.J Thomas

Copyright © 2023 Business Growth Publishers
All Rights Reserved

Contents

INTRODUCTION

Chapter 1
Developing a Business Idea

Chapter 2
Creating a Business Plan

Chapter 3
Securing Funding

Chapter 4
Building a Team

Chapter 5
Launching and Scaling

Chapter 6
Staying Ahead of the Game

Chapter 7
Conclusion

INTRODUCTION

"The Entrepreneur's Blueprint: A Step-by-Step Guide to Starting a New Business" is the ultimate guide for anyone looking to start their own business. Whether you're a first-time entrepreneur or a seasoned pro, this book provides a comprehensive overview of the key steps and strategies required to start and grow a successful business. From developing a business plan and securing funding, to building a team and launching your product or service, this book is packed with actionable advice and real-world examples to help you navigate the challenges and opportunities of starting a new business. With clear explanations, practical tips, and inspiring stories from successful entrepreneurs, "The Entrepreneur's Blueprint" is your go-to resource for turning your dream of starting a business into a reality.

Chapter 1

Developing a Business Idea

Identifying a problem or opportunity in the market
Conducting market research and validation
Defining your target audience and value proposition
Crafting a compelling elevator pitch

Starting a new business begins with a great idea. But where do you find that idea and how do you know if it's a good one? In this chapter, we'll explore the process of developing a business idea that has the potential to succeed in the marketplace.

First, it's important to understand that a great business idea is one that addresses a problem or opportunity in the market. This could be a product or service that fills a gap in the market, or a new way of solving an existing problem. To identify potential problems or opportunities, it's essential to conduct market research and validate your ideas. This can be done through surveys, interviews, and analysis of industry trends and data.

Once you have a clear understanding of the problem or opportunity you want to address, it's time to define your target audience and value proposition. Your target audience should be specific and well-defined, and your value proposition should clearly communicate how your product or service will solve the problem or meet the opportunity in the market.

Once you have a clear understanding of your target audience and value proposition, it's time to craft a compelling elevator pitch. This is a short and concise statement that describes your business idea and its value to potential customers. A great elevator pitch should be easy to understand, memorable, and convey the unique value of your product or service.

Developing a business idea is an iterative process and it may take several attempts before arriving at the final concept. The key is to keep testing and validating your ideas until you find one that truly resonates with your target audience and solves a problem or meets an opportunity in the market. With a solid business idea in hand, you're ready to move on to the next step of creating a business plan.

Chapter 2

Creating a Business Plan

Outlining your business model and revenue streams
Developing a marketing and sales strategy
Projecting financials and creating a budget
Identifying potential risks and mitigation strategies

A business plan is the roadmap for your business. It outlines your business model, revenue streams, marketing and sales strategy, financial projections, and more. A well-crafted business plan is essential for securing funding and communicating your vision to potential investors, partners, and employees.

In this chapter, we'll go through the process of creating a comprehensive business plan that will serve as a guide for starting and growing your business.

First, you'll want to outline your business model and revenue streams. This includes identifying how your business will make money, whether it be through product sales, subscriptions, advertising, or some other means. It's important to have a clear understanding of your revenue streams and how they align with your overall business strategy.

Next, you'll want to develop a marketing and sales strategy. This includes identifying your target audience, developing a positioning and messaging strategy, and outlining the tactics you'll use to reach and convert potential customers. A solid marketing and sales strategy is essential for driving growth and revenue.

It's also important to project your financials and create a budget. This includes forecasting your income and expenses, as well as identifying any potential risks and mitigation strategies. Financial projections will help you understand the financial viability of your business and make informed decisions about funding and growth.

Finally, it's important to review and update your business plan regularly as your business evolves. This will help you stay on track and make adjustments as needed. A business plan is a living document and should be updated as your business grows and changes.

A business plan is a crucial step in the process of starting a new business and will be an essential tool for securing funding and communicating your vision to potential investors, partners and employees. It will also serve as a guide for starting and growing your business.

Chapter 3

Securing Funding

Understanding the different types of funding available
Creating a fundraising plan and pitch deck
Networking and finding potential investors
Negotiating terms and closing a deal

Securing funding is a critical step in starting a new business. Without the necessary capital, it can be difficult to bring your business idea to life, build a team, and launch your product or service. In this chapter, we'll explore the different types of funding available and provide strategies for securing the capital you need to start and grow your business.

First, it's important to understand the different types of funding available. This includes traditional forms of financing such as bank loans and venture capital, as well as alternative forms of financing such as crowdfunding and angel investing. Each type of funding has its own advantages and disadvantages, and it's important to choose the right one for your business.

Once you have a clear understanding of the different types of funding available, it's time to create a fundraising plan and pitch deck. A fundraising plan outlines your fundraising goals, target investors, and timeline, while a pitch deck is a visual presentation that communicates your business idea, market opportunity, and financial projections to potential investors.

Networking and finding potential investors is also a key step in securing funding. This includes attending industry events, reaching out to angel investor groups and venture capital firms, and leveraging your personal and professional networks. Building relationships with potential investors takes time and effort, but it can be a valuable source of capital and mentorship for your business.

Finally, it's important to be prepared to negotiate terms and close a deal with investors. This includes understanding the terms of the funding, such as the equity you're giving up, as well as the rights and responsibilities of the investors. It's also important to have a legal representation to ensure that the deal is fair and protects your interests.

Securing funding is a critical step in starting a new business, and it's important to understand the different types of funding available, create a fundraising plan, find potential investors, and negotiate terms and close a deal. With the right funding in place, you'll have the resources you need to bring your business idea to life and build a successful business.

Chapter 4

Building a Team

Hiring employees and independent contractors
Finding the right co-founders and advisors
Building a culture and fostering collaboration
Managing and leading a team effectively

Building a team is an essential step in starting a new business. A great team can help you bring your business idea to life, overcome challenges, and drive growth. In this chapter, we'll explore the process of building a team, from hiring employees and independent contractors, to finding the right co-founders and advisors.

First, it's important to understand the different types of team members you'll need to bring your business idea to life. This includes full-time employees, part-time employees, independent contractors, and interns. Each type of team member has its own advantages and disadvantages, and it's important to choose the right one for your business.

When it comes to hiring employees, it's important to find the right fit for your business. This includes identifying the skills and experience needed for each role, as well as the cultural fit. It's also important to have a clear job description, and to conduct thorough interviews and background checks.

When it comes to finding the right co-founders and advisors, it's important to look for people with complementary skills and a shared vision for your business. Co-founders and advisors can provide valuable support and mentorship, and can help you navigate the challenges of starting a new business.

Once you have a team in place, it's important to build a culture and foster collaboration. This includes setting clear goals and expectations, as well as creating an environment that encourages creativity and innovation.

Finally, it's important to manage and lead your team effectively. This includes providing clear direction, setting goals and expectations, and providing feedback and recognition.

Building a team is an essential step in starting a new business. A great team can help you bring your business idea to life, overcome challenges, and drive growth. By understanding the different types of team members you'll need, finding the right fit, building a culture and fostering collaboration, and managing and leading your team effectively, you'll be able to build a successful team that will help you achieve your business goals.

Chapter 5

Launching and Scaling

Developing a product or service and testing it with customers
Creating a go-to-market strategy and executing on it
Building a brand and creating a strong online presence
Scaling the business and dealing with growth challenges

Launching and Scaling

Launching and scaling a business is the final step in bringing your business idea to life. In this chapter, we'll explore the process of launching and scaling a business, from developing a product or service and testing it with customers, to creating a go-to-market strategy and building a brand.

First, it's important to develop a product or service that meets the needs of your target audience. This includes conducting customer research, prototyping and testing, and iterating on your product or service until it meets the needs of your target audience.

Once your product or service is ready, it's time to create a go-to-market strategy. This includes identifying the channels you'll use to reach and convert potential customers, such as socialmedia, email marketing, or paid advertising. It's also important to create a messaging and positioning strategy that communicates the value of your product or service to your target audience.

It's also important to build a brand that reflects your business's values and resonates with your target audience. This includes creating a visual identity, developing a tone of voice, and building a strong online presence.

Scaling a business can be challenging, but it's important to have a plan in place to handle growth. This includes understanding your unit economics and scaling your marketing, sales, and customer service functions. It's also important to identify and prepare for potential scaling challenges, such as hiring more employees, managing more customers, and dealing with increased competition.

Launching and scaling a business is the final step in bringing your business idea to life. By developing a product or service that meets the needs of your target audience, creating a go-to-market strategy, building a brand, and handling growth challenges, you'll be able to launch and scale a successful business.

Chapter 6

Staying Ahead of the Game

Keeping up with industry trends and adapting to changes
Staying competitive and differentiating yourself from the competition
Continuously improving and innovating
Preparing for the future and positioning for exits or acquisitions

Starting a new business is just the beginning. To succeed in the long term, it's important to stay ahead of the game and anticipate changes in the marketplace. In this chapter, we'll explore strategies for staying competitive and positioning your business for success.

First, it's important to keep up with industry trends and adapt to changes. This includes staying informed about new technologies, market trends, and changes in consumer behavior. This will help you identify opportunities to innovate and stay ahead of the competition.

Next, it's important to differentiate yourself from the competition. This includes identifying your unique selling points, developing a unique brand and messaging, and finding ways to stand out in the marketplace.

It's also important to continuously improve andinnovate. This includes conducting customer research, testing new ideas, and iterating on your product or service. By continuously improving and innovating, you'll be able to stay ahead of the competition and better meet the needs of your target audience.

Finally, it's important to prepare for the future and position your business for success. This includes identifying potential exits or acquisitions, preparing for regulatory changes, and diversifying your revenue streams.

Staying ahead of the game is essential for the long-term success of your business. By keeping up with industry trends, differentiating yourself from the competition, continuously improving and innovating, and positioning your business for the future, you'll be able to build a sustainable and successful business.

Chapter 7

Conclusion

Summarizing key takeaways from the book
Encouraging the readers to take action and start their own business
Providing resources for further learning and support.

In conclusion, starting a new business is a challenging and rewarding journey. It takes hard work, perseverance, and the right mindset to turn a business idea into a reality. But with the right guidance and resources, it is possible to create a successful business that makes a positive impact on the world. We hope that this book has provided valuable insights and strategies for starting and growing a business, and that it has inspired readers to take action and pursue their entrepreneurial dreams. Remember, starting a business is not easy, but with the right mindset and guidance, anything is possible.

www.ingramcontent.com/pod-product-compliance
Lightning Source LLC
Chambersburg PA
CBHW050319220526
45465CB00005B/2047